"The poems of *Remembering the Sweetness* mark a yearning shared by all of us: the wish for tenderness, the need to have our lives punctuated by beauty, the hunger for a language dedicated to seeing into and beyond the rigmarole of our daily lives. This longing is, of course, driven by the more troubling aspects of personhood—misunderstanding, alienation, and the fragility of just about everything we know. Giantonio's carefully rendered poems are emblems of what sustains us."

—Tim Seibles, poet laureate of Virginia (2016-18) and author of *Fast Animal*, a finalist for the 2012 National Book Award

"In her debut collection, *Remember the Sweetness*, Polly Giantonio offers a deeply personal exploration of memory, family, and the fleeting moments that shape our lives. Through vivid imagery and tender reflection, she weaves a tapestry of ordinary yet profound experiences: a praying mantis at the doorstep, the first blueberry picked from a bush, a vigil by a father's bedside. With themes of loss, nostalgia, and quiet rebellion, Giantanio's poems invite us into the intimate spaces of life's small but significant moments—moments that echo long after they've passed. Whether meditating on the innocence of childhood or confronting the complexities of adulthood, *Remember the Sweetness* is a collection that speaks to the power of pause, the beauty in the overlooked, and the complexity of love."

—Jim Bennett, managing editor of Poetry Kit (poetrykit.org)

"To make small is not to break. To make small is not to lose. Polly Giantonio's poetry asks us to observe what translated Roland Barthes calls shadows' 'bits of.' The man's hand that presses into the woman's hip, 'each finger of your flower' and 'one anvil of dark / dirt under my nails' here telescope into the writer's best job: translating even the smallest letters—'d looked like b—u like n / w like m'—so they become a way to move a writer's hand against death and forgetfulness. Here's to the poet's mother's half-smoked cigarette, still smoldering in this fine collection."

—Terri Witek, Sullivan Chair in Creative Writing
and professor of English at Stetson University

"In *Remember the Sweetness* poet Polly Giantonio leaves behind the noise of ticker-tape chatter and reaches past the banal life of suburbia with its bookend beliefs. Her poems recognize a telling detail, how a praying mantis resembles an emerald queen, the way a tool handle picks up the polish of a maker, and a blueberry reveals the fullness of a season's sweetness. The world is seen through the eyes of an owl. We rise like a monarch from a chrysalis. Some of the strongest poems in this collection are ekphrastic, inspired, for example, by an Edward Hopper painting or Rodin's 'The Kiss.' Giantonio looks backward and now forward through an open window. We join her at the sill and breathe in the light."

—Gary W. Hawk,
author of *Into This Radiance, Kayaking Flathead Lake*

"Polly Giantonio's poems locate the spirit-hearts of ordinary moments. Traversing topics of nature and family, life and death, she examines the delicate chains of being we take for granted. Each poem, like the butterfly in the poem 'Liftoff,' climbs 'out of chrysalis' to do a celebratory dance, finding the beauty in the quotidian. Whether examining 'half naked trees with taffeta skirts', or recalling—without a flinch—her mother's 'head of chemo fuzz', Giantonio directs us to observe. Alongside her, we ignore our chirping phones to relish the smallest details of the everyday. By steering us away from the noise of the world, she gifts us with sweetness."

—Elizabeth Cohen, author of five poetry collections,
one short story collection, and the memoir
The Family on Beartown Road

Remember the Sweetness

Poems

Polly Giantonio

Rootstock Publishing
Montpelier, VT

Release Date: August 11, 2026

Paperback ISBN: 978-1-57869-399-3

Library of Congress Control Number: 2026907478

Published by Rootstock Publishing
an imprint of Ziggy Media, LLC
Montpelier, VT 05602
info@rootstockpublishing.com
www.rootstockpublishing.com

Cover art by Edgar Stewart of Edgar Stewart Design & Illustration (edgarstewart.com).
Book Interior and E-book Design by Amit Dey | amitdey2528@gmail.com

For reprint permissions or to schedule a poetry reading with the author, contact Polly at pgiantonio@gmail.com.

For Mom

Contents

The Praying Mantis

I find her on the deck by the front door
green as an emerald queen
her front legs folded in prayer

like a baby sleeping
with hands cupped together
at the crown of its head

mystics in meditation
they pray in the silent
smell of lilac

Blueberry Picking

from bushes that wintered
through snow and ice storms
long nights of the North

whose lichen-covered branches
leafed and grew
tiny pearls of earth-sugar
extracted from soil

I pick a blueberry
swollen with sun and water
that drops in my palm

a small bubble
that pops open with a bite
where the burst of juice oozes
between my teeth

but to be the toddler
blue stains on her cheeks
who gobbles—not one—

but palmfuls of berries
and croons for more

The Secret

after the painting by William-Adolphe Bouguereau

Her shoulder,
soft and full as a swan's breast,
illumines homely features
in graceful symmetry—
ivory beauty with reticent eyes
and full, sealed lips.
On the garden fountain ledge
a child idly circles
his finger in water,
while her sister whispers—
Father would be furious—
but what was it like?

Beyond

I dubbed out Mom's half-smoked Pall Mall—
It's not good for you, Mom. It makes me sick.
She wore navy shorts, a white polo
with a woven golf ball on a tee.

I'd been accepted to art schools
near San Francisco and close-to-home Philly.
Drawing excited me like when I sketched
a nude model with charcoal to capture a curve
of the calf or shadow below the breast.

I modeled naked for a modest fee—free of cheerleader-
A-student-class-dress-nicely-dope-smoking-baby-sitting-
dog-walking-clothes, my 15-year-old runner's body
posed empty and cold—a statue, a mold
of what they wanted me to be.

Life Drawing took my worries of a world at war
momentarily away. I craved to halt the ticker tape
of life's chatter, to solve a maze, seize the mystery
beyond a model's blue or brown iris.

I drifted in the music of Hendrix, Pink Floyd
to find a way out but it was a swim through seaweed
in a circle day after day—a robot programmed
by a suburbia of parents, teachers, news, trends.

On a clear September morning I said
goodbye to Mom, left her with her
smoldering cigarette, and cut
school to meet friends in the city.

Vigil at Father's Bed Before My Brother Arrives

Here we are. You.
Me on this hard chair
with the baby inside my womb
kicking.

Strong one
you said when you could still speak
the night you pulled the catheter out
'til a nurse heard the beeps.

Asleep tonight with morphine
in your shriveled form
knees folded in
toward your heart
protecting it from harm.

You're not my father
I shouted once in a teenage shitshow
aching to be heard above your baritone
that too often told me I was wrong
so at 17 I left
your home of bookend beliefs.

It never occurred to me you'd care.

Your son
is here now
I whisper in your ear
and the machine or you
sigh in relief.

Surprise

I was maybe 6, home sick, I sipped
ginger ale on the couch in the den
red bumps covered my face
arms, chest—scratching wasn't allowed

7 older kids were at school
tomatoes with basil simmered on the stove
mom answered the hallway phone
talked on and on about the flower show

outside a car engine shut off, our dog yipped
feet stomped up wooden steps from the garage
the door squeaked—*Sweet Pea*—he called
In the den, Daddy!

he loosened his tie, dropped his briefcase
pulled out a pack of Chuckles
red, green, yellow, orange, black—for me
Now close your eyes

I heard a paper bag—*Open!* his smile
showed the gap between his teeth
he handed me a box with a red rosebud –
under the lid were rows of chocolate

squares, circles, icing tops—once
when he wasn't working
he placed his palm over my gloved hand
to show me how to prune a rose

The Dandelion

Years before builders raped rolling hills
to build mini-mansions a few steps apart
I climbed a rope on a tree with roots
that reached to Middle Earth

I told secrets to white field mice
hummed to bullfrog songs
cursed my brothers who shot them
to watch their legs jump in salt

left home with a box of Cocoa Krispies
when I was 6   munched them by the stream
where the red fox ate our chickens
I kept watch under pink peonies

woke with screams and scenes of legs
on the floor   a carpet of black spiders
while Cold War soldiers marched
to scale the stone wall of my room

I hated when old man Max would scoop
me up to rub his whiskers on my cheek—
or when I went next door for sugar
a man with bushy brows and Cadillac

invited me for a ride
I was 4 or 5 with eyes o' blue
like those cherubs in paintings whose hair
curls like notes of "Moonlight Sonata"

I played black and white but where
was syncopation between?
when JFK was shot the nun stopped
we bowed our heads and prayed

the priests never quit their charades
with the boys lined up in white
I could go on and on about those priests
who listened to confessions

but never confessed
my father told me not to ask questions
so I went on a quest with Hermann Hesse
listened to Janis Joplin sing

old friends spun with LSD and weed
sped through money   joked at me
as if wanting peace
made me a freak

I ducked out of a sweat lodge
before my Vision Quest
into the cold lake where the universe
sparkled and spun my head

I birthed at home
hips hugging my newborn's skull
as he tried to escape the grip
that would bind us for life

my son is settled out West
we talk about coffees at night
far away but under the same moon
as my brother who died in my arms

stars lit midnight and time paused
birth in reverse he traveled
through the pelvic floor of death
the cosmos held its breath

his grasp released like a newborn
tearing away from the womb
my iris garden blooms in shades
gold purple peach and maroon

one anvil of dark
dirt under my nails
in the field of dandelions
milkweed pods and bees

For My Brother, Gary

1.
I crawled into your hideout
through brambles among maples and pines

from the pack of Pall Mall
you pulled a cigarette

while you dragged it crinkled red
a rabbit skittered nearby

I sputtered, coughed, nauseous
You'll be okay you promised
puffing Os round my head

2.
you understood trees
like a sculptor with his stone
knew the dignity of their reach

too proud to admit
d looked like b—u like n
w like m
you secretly asked me to read

3.
when the world misjudged you
Fuck them was your response
Come over for a pinch of Glenfiddich

we sipped by the woodstove
remembering when you were nine

dared me to the top of an oak
your fingers circled the sky
like the wingtips of a hawk—
you pictured yourself a pilot

4.
between breath and no-breath
you sway, ask so little—
in these last hours
you become soft

your withered back
a thin shield over
your damaged lungs

The Woman by the Window

after Cape Cod Morning by Edward Hopper

she appears slim in a poppy-orange dress
a 50s-style American housewife—
hair in a bun at the nape of her neck
inviting the touch of a tongue

from the window
she looks past a frame of gold
seagrass playing in the sun—
to the dunes and sea

she can't turn away
from two naked bodies
like the grass that bends and sways—
from outside the window's glare

obscures how she leans into their heat
strains to see what she cannot
to feel what might be

The Double Rainbow

Above the fields on Kibling Hill
a double rainbow glows
no bluebirds fly, no pots of gold

no lotteries won, no trumpets
blare or drums sound
an old woman shuts off water

a man stands from changing a flat
another stops emptying compost in a bin
to gaze at the display

the newborn at his mother's breast
both oblivious to the rainbow
fading in the rain-soaked sky

his eyes blink and fuse with hers
an instant's latch so strong
no locksmith can undo

she touches her index finger to his cheek
sings off tune—he quiets as if hearing
the harmony of Claire de Lune

A Moment with Mom Before Her Mirror

side by side on Mom's vanity bench
in front of her mirror framed in tiger wood
with a half dome of sunrays carved at the top
she holds my gaze in the glass

Always smile, Sweetheart

she pulls open the drawer
sectioned with jewelry
gifts from Dad or her father
rings left by her mother
she holds a string of pearls to her ashen neck
our eyes meet again in the reflection

You take these, you were with Dad
when he bought them for me

she places the long strand over my head
kisses my forehead
closes her eyes, hums to "Ave Maria"
playing in the room
the clock chimes two

she studies her image
touches her head of chemo fuzz

where once smooth waves of auburn curled

Color, that's what I need

she pulls a lipstick from the drawer
makes an O with her mouth as she paints it red

Ask them to use this, I want red lips for my viewing

she places the lipstick in my palm
closes my fingers, squeezes my hand

And the song, "Ave Maria," have someone sing along

Home

Fires torch acres of oak and pine
haze from out West drapes the sky
hides the sun and burns my eyes

how will my grandson thrive?
how do you survive
orange-gold butterfly?

buds on my stargazer lilies swell
without urging bees buzz
in a drunken dance around liatris

I ignore my chirping phone
in favor of the diving rock
at the pond that is warm

A Break in the Pandemic

time with my kids sliced from forward
held still by arms around each other
no radio, news, podcast, talk show

isolated where it's easy to forget
the next wall   the final exit

her voice   her hand in mine
it's been so long   I hold her
as if she were the last flower
in the desert

his blue-green eyes   long arms
that feeling from long ago
fear and excitement
of holding a newborn

their unmasked mouths
smiles   laughter releasing
the pandemic's gloom
how precisely

each makes a pour-over
for the other   around
a board game
that I lose

God's Walk

the screech of a red fox chills the air
where the river splits two bodies stop

a bodice hugs her breasts
that rise like wings with breath

her skin glows caramel from the moon
his shark-gray skin, a camouflage

his bat-like eyes avert her gaze
a second screech warns—his presence

unearths demons hidden in the core
an army greater than Sauron's

takes lives like a machine pulverizes waste
he rouses people to believe they're supreme

her round belly pulses
with a movement in her womb

as he leaves he proclaims—*I am a virus*
that will mutate and survive

Wasted

the unbroken *whirr* of wasps on wood
heifers munch and deadstare
crows *rwaark* in pairs

a time when sorrow gathers
forces—the TV clamors
with shouts and screams

she draws a deep breath
and strength from weed
as if sucking another drop

she empties into water
even before her first moonblood
her unsettled spirit fractures

like a prism fractures colors
orange-yellow flowers
splash her minidress

An Unknown Land

It's dusk when Owl swoops to perch
on a leafless branch—stares
to pause in a haze of loss

when she flies again, her eyes span
beyond what anyone can see—
a mouse scurrying through grass

double rainbows no one believes
encircling home. The child's smile
persists even as I wonder

if she'll hear the morning rise with predawn birds
will the stream where heron hunts still run clear?
will the black mink be extinct?

Solstice

remember the sweetness
of viburnum blossoms
ghosts from the grave
drifting in a draft

a dump truck roars through the valley
its engine grinds to a lower gear
the growl grows louder
as it lurches uphill

through the whiteout
numb with cold
ice freezes the door
of the snow-banked car

Liftoff

she climbs out of her chrysalis
dangles dangerously on the tip
of her shedding

wrestles her leg free
from fibers that encased her
flaps a wing   then with great effort

pulls herself over the wooden step
onto the deck   drags her orange-gold
and black cape as if in procession

until she points her wings upward
rises   flutters   floats weightless
toward the sky

I too climb   over the edge
of a wicker basket
below the open balloon

flames expand the vacuum
as it bumps along packed earth
until suddenly   my lungs fill

fan out in wing-like fashion   I rise
toss each regret over the side
into a free fall   down

down   crashing through air
until they dive deep into dirt
where heifers stomp

October's Confetti

frogs' groans, goldfinch songs—gone
fallen into a hmmm through the fields

hints of ripe-fleshed pears powder the air
ghosts chase squirrels through forest musk

half-naked trees with taffeta skirts
rustle in a gust   apricot, gold, chili-pepper

red hillsides of Jackson-Pollock splash
gold baubles shimmer—trunks like upright tubes

scarlet explodes into a climax
only the moss remains steadfast and green

earthworms halt garden work
to burrow down   a lone leaf glides

other leaves flutter like anxious eyes
or crinkle-crack in tap-dance style

On an Ordinary Morning

pale orange sunlight bathes Snickers
the old barn cat sprawled on snow
I've come to find an unfamiliar tool

in a workshop where years ago
a young apprentice studied burning steel
how to stretch, bend or crease the ore

his name stamp in the chimney groove
I trace each raised letter
blow away dust as if to wake him

hear his hammer on anvil again
a hundred horseshoes brown with rust
hang from beams—his tools spread on walls

the creaser he forged lay on the work table
its handle polished by his calloused palms
I close the doors and leave this quiet forge

draft 2

I was 50ish when I began
to write and already my mind
had slowed   maybe because
of stress from the divorce

then a breakup   then my brother's
death then my mother's   I wrote
about birth(ing) and departures
as juice dribbled down my chin

when I bit a pear I thought
these moments broke me
open the writing followed
suit but my teacher blasted

the poems in class   after that
I had a lot of sex with a cowboy
(and stopped writing) for a while
until I began again

After Seeing Rodin at the Met

we walk to Bemelmen's Bar
in the Carlyle Hotel styled with murals
elephants skating and rabbits picnicking

live piano and jazz   low lights
on Sunday afternoon the luster of amber
in the coupe cocktail glass

with each sip of his Manhattan
his features soften like warm
honey beside a fire

Winter Thaw

after coyote, fox, bear
left their marks
you pretended not to see

before the storm
leaves turned golden
buttons down your chest

after the leaves fell
you undid each button
before bats found home

and the snow's white
built a wall
on the tree branch

I touched your breast
after loneliness panted
red embers in the wood stove

burned to ash
before the grass turned green
you walked barefoot

in the stream bed
after snow
began to melt

Peony

As if war departs with the pink of morning sun, your fragrance possesses the earth and air. A current of unstoppable ants, silent and determined, climb stems, drawn to your yellow core. Buoyed from burdens as if a hail storm could not doom your existence. Each finger of your flower unfolds a rainbow of fuchsia.

A dark cloud casts a net that stalls your perfume. Rain collects on your petals like drops in an open palm. A flash of lightning freezes your form in light. Heavy now, your head droops but in beauty.

The Kiss and the Caterpillar

after Rodin's The Kiss

In the middle of a gallery
the mother's hand sweats
swollen and warm clutching her child.

They walk around
the naked man and woman
and stop in front of the woman's breast.

The mother fixes her eyes on the man's hand
that presses into the woman's hip like he's pulling
a full bag of food across a counter

while her son reaches for a caterpillar
rippling in a groove on rough marble
where it moves below the man's big toe.

The Last Visit

through the hiss of oxygen
a stale smell of sweat mixed with cleaner
machines to measure vitals roll past his door

his head is bent to the side
eyelashes crusted in white
he raises his brows
tries to say
"beau—ti—ful"
but   suffocates in congestion
his eyes   glazed with defeat   look at me
or through me to fix on the wall
        unblinking

a doctor and nurse burst in
with smiles as if my brother belongs to them
        his eyes widen   fasten to mine
his eyebrows furrow
        in terror
he moves his head   pleads "no"
        I tell them to leave

"they're coming" he mouths

        I won't let them hurt you
and hold his trembling hand
in the silence between us
        a gulf

I empty my thoughts
        surround us in a shield
where fists from long ago cannot reach
where failure does not exist
where trapped in a sinking submarine is erased
        I will his shame to burn away
and his heart to be   freed
from danger

his eyeballs move   pause   move   stop
like slivers of light through shutters   his life peaks
then his eyelids shut

we are children again   at the edge of our pond
he shows me how to hold a stone   flick my wrist
his stones skim like dancers across the surface
but my skips sink into nothing next to his

Acknowledgments

Many thanks to the editors of the following publications in which versions of these poems appeared:

The Café Review, *The Ekphrastic Review*, "The Secret"
Caught in the Net, "God's Walk"
Comstock Review, "The Woman by the Window"
Dawntreader, "An Unknown Land" and "Winter Thaw"
Sarasvati, "Peony"
County Lines, A Literary Journal, "Vigil at Father's Bed Before My Brother Arrives"

I am most grateful to Jim Bennett whose guidance and feedback nurtured my writing and inspired me to create this book.

My thanks to Samantha and her staff at Rootstock Publishing for their professional expertise.

I would like to express my love and appreciation to my late parents, Polly and John, whose unwavering love resides with me every day. And to my husband, Marc, and my children, Chelsea and Zach, who encouraged and supported me and never shied away from my drafts.

About the Author

Polly Giantonio is a writer and workshop facilitator. Her search for inner peace led her along an unconventional path from the age of sixteen. She completed her undergraduate and master's degrees later in life while raising her children. Her poems and work have appeared in various journals including the *Comstock Review*, *Café Review*, and *Poets & Writers*. She has worked as a content creator and editor. As a trained Amherst Writers and Artists facilitator, she has worked closely with the Vermont Arts Council, the Central Vermont Council on Aging, and the Vermont Community Foundation to offer local writing workshops. She lives in rural Vermont.

www.ingramcontent.com/pod-product-compliance
Lightning Source LLC
Chambersburg PA
CBHW032248270826
50566CB00023B/164
9781578693993